REBEL GIRLS LEAD

D0953905

25 TALES OF POWERFUL WOMEN

Good Night Stories for Rebel Girls and Rebel Girls are registered trademarks. Good Night Stories for Rebel Girls and all other Rebel Girls titles are available for bulk purchase for sale promotions, premiums, fundraising, and educational needs. For details, write to sales@rebelgirls.com.

This is a work of creative nonfiction. It is a collection of heartwarming and thought-provoking stories inspired by the life and adventures of twenty-five influential women. It is not an encyclopedic account of the events and accomplishments of their lives.

www.rebelgirls.com

Parts of this work have been previously published in the books *Good Night Stories for Rebel Girls*, *Good Night Stories for Rebel Girls 2,* and *Good Night Stories for Rebel Girls: 100 Immigrant Women Who Changed the World.*

Created by Francesca Cavallo and Elena Favilli
Additional text by Abby Sher, Sarah Parvis, Jestine Ware, and Andrea Debbink
Art direction by Giulia Flamini
Cover illustrations and graphic design by Annalisa Ventura

Printed in Canada, December 2020
10 9 8 7 6 5 4 3 2 1
ISBN: 978-1-953424-06-8

CONTENTS

FOREWORD

Dear Rebel,

When Kamala Harris was elected as the first female vice president of the United States, making her the highest-ranking woman elected in US history, it was a cause for celebration for rebel girls everywhere. Another glass ceiling was shattered. Kamala represents all that women can accomplish, and coming from a mixed Jamaican and South Asian heritage, she also represents the wonderful diversity of the United States.

Here at Rebel Girls, we took a moment to reflect on this historic first and started plotting how we could celebrate appropriately. We wanted to share Kamala's inspiring story, as well as other stories of contemporary women who are leading the way— leaders like Stacey Abrams, who has been working tirelessly to protect and register voters, and Jacinda Ardern, who has deftly steered New Zealand through the coronavirus pandemic.

To complement the stories of these phenomenal women, we decided to collect stories of beloved leaders from our first three volumes of *Good Night Stories for Rebel Girls*, such as Malala Yousafzai, Ruth Bader Ginsburg, and Michelle Obama. With *Rebel Girls Lead*, we want to showcase and honor the courage, ingenuity, and resilience of these rebel women. Each of them use their energy, talents, and enormous hearts to lead the way in government, activism, sports, business, and more.

In this mini edition, you will learn about legendary basketball coach Pat Summitt, who challenged and uplifted her players every day; Wilma Mankiller, who transformed her community as the first female head of the Cherokee Nation; and Xiye Bastida, whose incredible journey as a climate activist is just beginning.

The women in this book started out just like you. They were kids who had dreams and fears, hopes and questions. They were full of curiosity and a desire to make a difference. They faced challenges, and they kept going. And the world will remember them for their leadership.

As you move through the world, remember that you, too, are powerful. You can speak up for the things that matter to you. You can rally people together, and you can find solutions to fix things that are broken. You can be a leader.

Believe in yourself, and know that you are part of a strong, supportive community of rebel girls worldwide. We are cheering for you.

Stay Rebel!

Jes Wolfe
CEO, Rebel Girls

ALY RAISMAN

GYMNAST AND TEAM CAPTAIN

Once there was a girl named Aly who found magic inside every sunrise. Aly saw the sun rise a lot, because she got up early to practice her cartwheels, jumps, and round-offs. From the time she could walk, she was in love with gymnastics.

When she turned ten, Aly told her coaches, "I'm going to go to the Olympics, and I'm gonna win floor." She had just met these new coaches a few days before. But they took one look at her bright, determined face and knew she meant business. A few years later, she began collecting gold medals in major competitions. She flipped and vaulted, soaring through the air in glittering leotards. Her favorite routines were on the floor, where she danced and leaped with a huge smile.

In 2012, Aly made her dreams come true. She was going to the Olympics! She and her incredible teammates were nicknamed the "Fierce Five." And these fierce gymnasts chose her to be their team captain. Being a gymnastics team captain is challenging. The athletes compete together to win team medals. But they also compete against one another for individual medals.

Aly did her best to bring out the strongest performance in each member of the team. She knew when to give a teammate space, when to give a pep talk, and when to tell them all to take a nap.

Her efforts paid off. Aly won a gold medal for her floor exercise, and she led the team to a gold medal, too. And four years later, Captain Aly went back to the Olympics and did it again. She won six more medals! Through it all, she says, "It is the journey and not the destination that really matters."

BORN MAY 25, 1994
UNITED STATES OF AMERICA

ANGELA MERKEL

CHANCELLOR

Once upon a time, in Templin, Germany, there lived a seven-year-old girl named Angela. One Sunday, she was listening to her father's sermon in church when her mother started to cry.

"What's the matter?" Angela asked.

"They are going to build a wall," her mother said. "They want to seal off the border between East Germany and West Germany."

Angela was stunned. "Why would they build a wall?" she thought. "People should be free to go wherever they like."

The Berlin Wall prevented East Germans from going to the West. They were also barred from listening to the news coming from the other side.

Every day, Angela hid in the school bathroom with a little radio. It was illegal to listen to stations from the West. But she didn't care. She wanted to know what was happening in her country!

When Angela grew up, she studied chemistry. She wanted to become a university professor. But the government had a special force known as the secret police. They told Angela that she would be promoted, but only if she spied on others. Angela refused. She never became a professor.

She was working as a researcher in a lab in 1989 when the Berlin Wall was demolished. She called her mom and said, "I think we're free to go to the West." Indeed, they were.

Angela eventually became chancellor of Germany—the head of the whole country! She is a determined leader who knows the pain that walls can cause. She never wants her people to be divided again.

BORN JULY 17, 1954
GERMANY

"AS LONG AS YOU HAVE ONE PERSON WHO BELIEVES IN YOU . . . THERE'S A LOT OF MAGIC IN THAT."
—ALY RAISMAN

ILLUSTRATION BY SALINI PERERA

"WHAT WE SEEK IS HARMONY AMONG NATIONS. THAT WAS AND REMAINS THE GREATEST GOAL OF EUROPEAN UNITY."
—ANGELA MERKEL

ILLUSTRATION BY ELENIA BERETTA

ANN RICHARDS

GOVERNOR

When Ann was a little girl, her father taught her to hunt and fish and tell great stories.

In high school, she became an expert debater. Her talents and quick wit even scored her a debate scholarship to college.

After she got married, she and her husband attended rallies and spoke out in support of equal rights for women and people of color.

In her home, Ann hosted rowdy pool parties and spirited dinners. Sometimes she would greet her guests in wild costumes! She was clever and charming, and everyone wanted to be near her.

But she was growing restless. She was a stay-at-home mom with four children. "I was so bored cooking and sewing," Ann said. She needed more.

She started her career in politics by helping another woman win a local election. And, in 1975, friends convinced her to run for her first office: county commissioner. She won and threw herself into her work. Next up, she became state treasurer.

Ann was shocked when she was invited to give the keynote speech at the 1988 Democratic National Convention. She cracked jokes and spoke about the needs of working people and her hopes for the future. Suddenly, the whole country knew her name!

In 1990, she became governor of Texas. In her single term, she appointed women, Black people, Latinx people, and people with disabilities to positions of power. She did not accomplish everything she set out to do. But she made sure that children of all kinds could see people who looked like them in government.

SEPTEMBER 1, 1933–SEPTEMBER 13, 2006
UNITED STATES OF AMERICA

"I DID NOT WANT MY
TOMBSTONE TO READ, 'SHE
KEPT A REALLY CLEAN HOUSE.'
I THINK I'D LIKE THEM TO
REMEMBER ME BY SAYING,
'SHE OPENED GOVERNMENT
TO EVERYONE.'"
—ANN RICHARDS

CLEOPATRA

PHARAOH

Once upon a time, in ancient Egypt, a pharaoh died. He left his kingdom to his ten-year-old son, Ptolemy XIII, and to his eighteen-year-old daughter, Cleopatra.

The two had very different ideas about how to run the country. Soon Cleopatra was kicked out of the palace! A civil war broke out.

Julius Caesar, the emperor of Rome, traveled to Egypt. He wanted to help Cleopatra and Ptolemy come to an agreement. "If only I could meet Caesar before my brother does," Cleopatra thought. "I could convince him that I'm the better pharaoh."

But she was banished from the palace! The guards would never let her in.

Cleopatra asked her servants to roll her up inside a carpet and smuggle her into Caesar's rooms. Impressed by her daring, Caesar restored Cleopatra to the throne. They became a couple and had a son. Cleopatra moved to Rome but returned to Egypt after Caesar was killed.

The new Roman leader, Mark Antony, heard a lot about this strong Egyptian queen. He wanted to meet her. This time, she arrived on a golden barge, surrounded by precious jewels and silk.

It was love at first sight.

Cleopatra and Mark Antony were inseparable. They had three children and loved each other to the end of their lives.

When Cleopatra died, the empire ended with her. She was the last pharaoh to rule ancient Egypt.

69 BCE–AUGUST 12, 30 BCE

EGYPT

ILLUSTRATION BY
KIKI LJUNG

"I WILL NOT BE
TRIUMPHED
OVER."
—CLEOPATRA

ELIZABETH I

QUEEN

A long time ago, in England, there was a king who wanted to leave his kingdom to a son.

When his wife gave birth to a daughter, King Henry VIII was so mad that he left her. He sent the child away and married another woman. He believed that only a man would be able to rule the country after he died. So he was delighted when his new wife gave birth to a boy, Edward.

Henry's daughter Elizabeth grew up a bright and brilliant girl, with striking red hair and a fiery temper.

Edward was only nine years old when his father died and he became king. A few years later, he also became ill and died. Edward's half-sister Mary then became queen. Mary thought that Elizabeth was plotting against her. So she locked Elizabeth in the Tower of London!

One day, the Tower guards burst into her cell. "The Queen is dead," they shouted. And then they fell to their knees in front of her. Elizabeth instantly went from being a prisoner in the Tower to the country's new queen.

Elizabeth's court was home to musicians, poets, painters, and playwrights. The most famous was William Shakespeare, whose plays Elizabeth adored. She wore gowns decorated with pearls and lace. She never married. She valued her own independence as highly as that of her country.

Her people loved her dearly. When she died, Londoners took to the streets to mourn the greatest queen they had ever known.

SEPTEMBER 7, 1533–MARCH 24, 1603
ENGLAND

ILLUSTRATION BY
ANA GALVAN

"A CLEAR AND
INNOCENT CONSCIENCE
FEARS NOTHING."
—ELIZABETH 1

EUFROSINA CRUZ

ACTIVIST AND POLITICIAN

Once there was a girl who didn't want to make tortillas.

When her father told her that women can only make tortillas and children, she burst into tears. She promised to show him that it wasn't true. "You can leave this house, but don't expect a single cent from me," he told her.

Eufrosina started out by selling chewing gum and fruit on the street. She used the money to pay for her studies. She got a degree in accounting and returned home. She started to teach young Indigenous girls like herself so they could find the strength to build their own lives, too.

One day, she decided to run for mayor of her town. She won many votes, but the townsmen canceled the election. "A woman as mayor? No way," they said.

Furious, Eufrosina went to work. She founded an organization called QUIEGO to help Indigenous women fight for their rights. Their symbol was a white lily. "Wherever I go, I take this flower to remind people that Indigenous women are exactly like that: natural, beautiful, and resilient," Eufrosina said.

A few years later, she became the first Indigenous woman to be elected president of the Oaxacan state congress. When the First Lady of Mexico came to visit, Eufrosina walked arm in arm with her.

She showed her father—and the whole world—that there is nothing the strong Indigenous women of Mexico cannot do.

BORN JANUARY 1, 1979
MEXICO

"WHEN A WOMAN DECIDES TO CHANGE, EVERYTHING CHANGES AROUND HER."
—EUFROSINA CRUZ

ILLUSTRATION BY PAOLA ROLLO

GIUSI NICOLINI

MAYOR

There was a young woman named Giusi who loved the little island of Lampedusa. Criminal groups and ruthless corporations wanted to build hotels and vacation homes there. But that would destroy Lampedusa's pristine beaches! So Giusi wouldn't let them.

She was the director of Lampedusa's nature reserve. "It is my duty to protect this island with all my might," she said. Her enemies burned down her father's shop. "You will not intimidate me," she declared. Her car and her boyfriend's van were set on fire. "I will not back down!" she said.

Lampedusa is a tiny island in the Mediterranean Sea, between Europe and Africa. Many refugees landed there. They were fleeing Africa to escape war and build a better life in Europe. The inhabitants of Lampedusa didn't know what to do. "Should we send these people back to protect our island?" they wondered. "Or should we welcome them?"

With these questions in mind, they voted for their next mayor.

Giusi was one of five candidates. People knew she had given all she had to protect the island in the past. They wanted to hear what she thought about the refugees. Giusi explained her point of view with four simple words: "Protect people, not borders."

Lampedusans elected her.

As mayor, Giusi reorganized the island's immigration center to be able to welcome as many people as possible. "We want to see many boats on our shores," she insisted, "because that will mean that these people made it here and didn't drown."

BORN MARCH 5, 1961
ITALY

"IT'S NATURAL FOR AN ISLAND
TO BE WELCOMING!"
—GIUSI NICOLINI

ILLUSTRATION BY
LAURA PÉREZ

HARRIET TUBMAN

FREEDOM FIGHTER

One day, a girl was standing in front of a grocery store when a Black man came running past. He was being chased by a white man. The white man yelled, "Stop that man! He's my slave!"

She did nothing. The girl's name was Araminta, and she was twelve years old. She was also enslaved. She hoped the man would escape.

Just then, the overseer hurled a heavy object at the running man. He missed and hit Araminta on the head instead. She was badly injured. But her thick hair cushioned the blow enough to save her life. "My hair had never been combed," she said, "and it stood out like a bushel basket."

A few years later, she married a man named John Tubman. She changed her name to Harriet after her mother. Then the family who owned her put her up for sale. So Harriet decided to escape.

Harriet hid in the daytime and traveled by night. When she crossed the border into Pennsylvania, she realized for the first time in her life she was free. "I looked at my hands to see if I was the same person now that I was free," she said. "There was such a glory over everything. . . . I felt like I was in heaven."

She thought about the runaway slave and her family in Maryland who were still enslaved. She knew she had to help them. Over the next eleven years, she went back nineteen times and rescued hundreds of enslaved people.

She was never captured, and she never lost a single person.

CIRCA 1822–MARCH 10, 1913
UNITED STATES OF AMERICA

ILLUSTRATION BY
SALLY NIXON

"EVERY GREAT DREAM BEGINS WITH
A DREAMER. ALWAYS REMEMBER, YOU
HAVE WITHIN YOU THE STRENGTH,
THE PATIENCE, AND THE PASSION TO
REACH FOR THE STARS TO CHANGE
THE WORLD."
—HARRIET TUBMAN

JACINDA ARDERN

PRIME MINISTER

Jacinda grew up on an apple farm in New Zealand. She lived with her family, her pet sheep Reggie, and her deep belief that girls can do anything.

She drove a tractor and worked at a fish-and-chips shop. She also loved DJing music and thought about being a scientist. But Jacinda saw how many of her neighbors didn't have enough money to buy food or shoes. She wanted to help them. So she went into politics.

After Jacinda graduated from university, she worked for Helen Clark, the first woman to be elected prime minister in the country. Later, Jacinda became the youngest member of the House of Representatives and was elected the leader of the Labour Party. People were excited about her strength and optimism. Fans buzzed around her. The media wrote all about "Jacindamania." On October 26, 2017, when she was just thirty-seven years old, Jacinda became prime minister of New Zealand!

Her first term in office was difficult. There was a terrible attack on two mosques and a deadly volcano eruption. Then the global coronavirus pandemic began.

Every time Jacinda faced a tragedy, she made sure the whole country felt like she was standing with them. She wore a headscarf called a *hijab* to mourn with Muslims. She changed gun laws so people would be safer. She called for a national lockdown to keep people from getting sick during the pandemic. But she also assured the little children of New Zealand that the tooth fairy would still be allowed to fly! Jacinda's motto has always been "Be strong, be kind." And that's exactly what she is.

BORN JULY 26, 1980
NEW ZEALAND

ILLUSTRATION BY
AISHA AKEJU

"IN THESE TOUGH TIMES, WE'VE SEEN
THE BEST OF US. WE'VE BEEN ABLE TO
CLEAR HIGH HURDLES AND FACE HUGE
CHALLENGES BECAUSE OF WHO WE ARE,
AND BECAUSE WE HAD A PLAN."
—JACINDA ARDERN

KAMALA HARRIS

VICE PRESIDENT

O nce upon a time, there was a girl who attended civil rights marches before she was even born. Later, her parents, who were originally from India and Jamaica, took her to protests. They shouted chants while wide-eyed Kamala watched from her stroller.

Eventually, Kamala outgrew the stroller and ventured onto the streets of Oakland, California, on her own. She knew she wanted to be someone who could help others in times of trouble.

Kamala went to Howard University, in Washington, DC, and followed in the footsteps of many famous Black lawyers who came before her. She took an internship on Capitol Hill. Every day, she walked by the Supreme Court building. On it, the words "Equal Justice Under Law" were etched into the stone. Kamala thought about how to make sure those words were true for everybody.

She followed her dreams and became a lawyer. In the courtroom, she always asked tough questions, battling against fierce adversaries with her words. Kamala demanded that people listen to her.

She decided to run for office. She became the first-ever female district attorney in the San Francisco Bay Area, beating out her old boss to land the job. She later ran for attorney general of the whole state of California—and won!

Then Kamala climbed even higher. She was elected to the United States Senate. And, in 2020, former vice president Joe Biden chose her as his running mate when he ran for president. The powerful pair won the election, and Kamala became the first woman and the first person of color to ever hold that office.

BORN OCTOBER 20, 1964
UNITED STATES OF AMERICA

ILLUSTRATION BY
NICOLE MILES

"WHILE I MAY BE THE
FIRST WOMAN IN THIS
OFFICE, I WON'T BE
THE LAST."
—KAMALA HARRIS

LADY GAGA

Once there was a girl named Stefani who needed music to survive. At school, she was bullied. At home, she fought with her dad. But at the piano, belting out her own songs, she felt like she could change the world.

She started playing piano when she was four years old and was performing in a New York City nightclub by the time she was fourteen. Stefani was dedicated. She studied music and performance. She created her own songs and dreamed up her own style. She was loud, bright, and fierce. Onstage, she wore bedazzled bikinis, face paint, and wigs. And she called herself Lady Gaga.

In 2008, Lady Gaga released her first single. People loved it! Her next hit song topped the charts in many countries. As she got more and more popular, her outfits and performances got wilder. One time, she dove from the roof of a football stadium. Another time, she wore a dress made of raw meat!

But as she got older, Lady Gaga realized, "The most shocking thing I can possibly do is be completely vulnerable and honest." She started talking to the press about how she was abused as a teenager and was in treatment to deal with her trauma.

Lady Gaga wanted to be there for other people who were hurting, too. She started the Born This Way Foundation, which helps young people talk about mental illness. She encouraged everyone to spread acts of kindness.

When Covid-19 struck, she helped organize a worldwide online concert to raise money to fight the pandemic and, most importantly, to share the gift of music.

BORN MARCH 28, 1986
UNITED STATES OF AMERICA

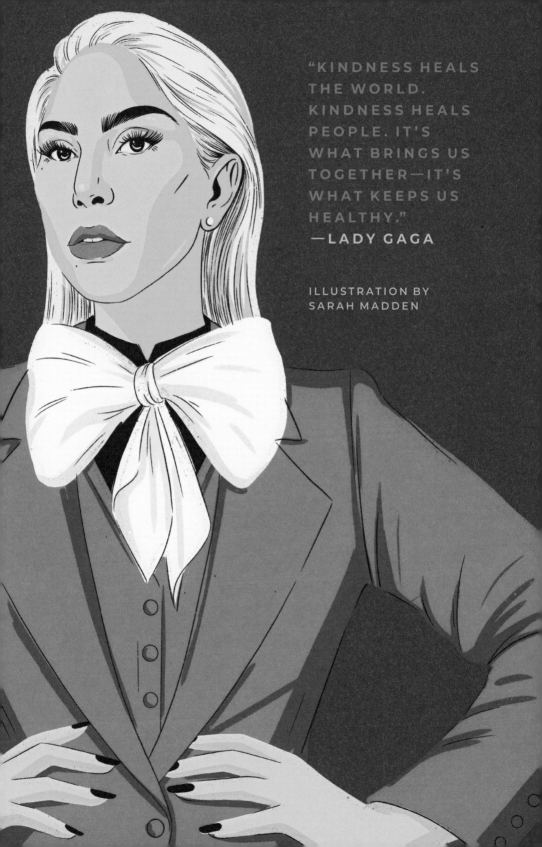

"KINDNESS HEALS THE WORLD. KINDNESS HEALS PEOPLE. IT'S WHAT BRINGS US TOGETHER—IT'S WHAT KEEPS US HEALTHY."
—LADY GAGA

ILLUSTRATION BY SARAH MADDEN

LEYMAH GBOWEE

PEACE ACTIVIST

Once, in Liberia, a woman stopped a war. Her name was Leymah, and she was a single mother of four. Her country was going through a terrible civil war. Children were becoming soldiers. And hundreds of thousands of people were dying. Leymah did everything she could to help those who had been traumatized by the fighting.

One day, she was invited to a conference organized by the West Africa Network for Peacebuilding. "Women like me had come from almost all eighteen countries in West Africa," Leymah recalled.

At the conference, she learned about conflict and conflict resolution. The women shared their experiences and talked about what war had taken from their lives. For Leymah, it was eye-opening. "No one else is doing this—focusing only on women and only on building peace," she thought.

She became the leader of a program called the Women in Peacebuilding Network. She recruited other women to help, too. She went to mosques for Friday afternoon prayers, to markets on Saturday mornings, and to churches every Sunday. All the women she spoke to wanted the war to end.

Leymah and the other women in her network pressured the groups that were fighting to start peace talks. Then they gathered in front of the hotel where the negotiations were taking place and demanded progress. They even blocked the hotel exit to keep the negotiators from leaving until they had reached a deal.

When the Liberian civil war ended, Leymah was awarded the Nobel Peace Prize. "When women gather," she says, "great things will happen."

BORN FEBRUARY 1, 1972

LIBERIA

ILLUSTRATION BY
THANDIWE TSHABALALA

"WE MUST CONTINUE TO
UNITE IN SISTERHOOD TO TURN
OUR TEARS INTO TRIUMPH."
—LEYMAH GBOWEE

MALALA YOUSAFZAI

EDUCATION ACTIVIST

Once there was a girl who loved school. Her name was Malala. Malala lived in a peaceful valley in Pakistan. One day, a group of armed men called the Taliban took control of the valley. They frightened people with their guns.

The Taliban forbade girls from going to school. Many people disagreed, but they thought it would be safer to keep their girls at home.

Malala thought this was unfair and wrote about it online. She loved school very much. So one day, she said on TV, "Education is power for women. The Taliban are closing girls' schools because they don't want women to be powerful."

A short while later, Malala got onto her school bus as usual. Suddenly, two Taliban men stopped the bus and shouted, "Which one of you is Malala?"

When her friends looked at her, the men fired their guns, hitting her in the head and injuring two other girls as well.

Malala was rushed to the hospital, but she did not die. Thousands of children sent her get well cards, and she recovered faster than anyone could have imagined.

"They thought bullets would silence us, but they failed," she said. "Let us pick up our books and our pens. They are our most powerful weapons. One child, one teacher, one book, and one pen can change the world."

Malala is the youngest person ever to receive the Nobel Peace Prize.

BORN JULY 12, 1997
PAKISTAN

"WHEN THE WHOLE WORLD IS SILENT, EVEN ONE VOICE BECOMES POWERFUL."
—MALALA YOUSAFZAI

ILLUSTRATION BY SARA BONDI

MARY BARRA

CEO

As far back as Mary could remember, she loved cars. Her cousin had a fiery red convertible. And, at ten years old, she knew she wanted one, too.

Lucky for her, she grew up in a car town. She lived near Detroit. Nicknamed "Motor City," Detroit was where cars were made in the United States. Her father worked at a General Motors, or GM, factory. And Mary followed in his footsteps.

In addition to cars, she loved math and science. Her parents wisely encouraged her to keep studying what she liked. That's how she found engineering. It's the type of science that deals with designing and building things. A car, a bridge, a tunnel, a dam, and a stadium are all designed by engineers.

Few girls studied engineering, but Mary did. While still in school, she got her first job at GM. She inspected cars on an assembly line. Later, the company paid for Mary to get a business degree. Over the years, she held jobs in many different departments at GM. She was clever and straightforward. She easily mastered new tasks and kept moving up.

In 2014, she was named the CEO, or chief executive officer, of GM. Mary was the first woman to head a major auto company. And she led GM through good times and tough times.

"As engineers, scientists, and inventors, we get to imagine what's next and then make it happen," Mary said. As CEO, she invested in cars that run on electricity instead of gas and even cars that could drive themselves. She learned everything about the company and the business so she could make the cars of the future.

BORN DECEMBER 24, 1961
UNITED STATES OF AMERICA

ILLUSTRATION BY
FANESHA FABRE

"IF YOU HAVE A PROBLEM, YOU'VE
GOT TO SOLVE IT. BECAUSE THAT
PROBLEM IS GOING TO GET BIGGER
IN SIX MONTHS."
—MARY BARRA

MELINDA GATES

PHILANTHROPIST

Once upon a time, a girl dreamed of using technology to make the world a better place.

At school, Melinda adored her teacher, Mrs. Bauer, who convinced the school to build a computer lab. Melinda loved the lab and all the shiny computers, but most of all, she loved coding because it felt like solving a puzzle.

In college, she stayed up late coding in her school's spooky old basement. She and her friends held contests: who could program the fastest with the fewest mistakes? The loser had to touch the frog specimens in the biology lab!

New software programs were released every year. Melinda wanted to be part of it, so after college she worked at a small computer company called Microsoft. That small company grew into a giant one.

When Melinda met the company's co-founder, Bill Gates, she found out that he was funny, also loved puzzles, and shared her dream of improving the world. They eventually fell in love and got married. After having their first daughter, Melinda quit her job to focus on philanthropy, or giving her time and money to help others. She wanted to create real, lasting change.

"Where should we start?" asked Bill.

"I want to help every girl make her dreams come true," she replied. "When women and girls are treated equally, life is better for everyone— men and boys, too."

Melinda decided she would provide women and girls with greater access to healthcare, education, and jobs. Together, she and Bill created the largest philanthropic organization in the world.

BORN AUGUST 15, 1964
UNITED STATES OF AMERICA

ILLUSTRATION BY
ANNALISA VENTURA

"WHEN WE INVEST IN WOMEN AND GIRLS,
WE ARE INVESTING IN THE PEOPLE WHO
INVEST IN EVERYONE ELSE."
—MELINDA GATES

MICHELLE OBAMA

LAWYER AND FIRST LADY

Once upon a time, there was a girl who was always afraid. Her name was Michelle Robinson, and she lived in a tiny apartment in Chicago with her family.

"Maybe I'm not smart enough," she worried. "Maybe I'm not good enough." And her mother would say, "If it can be done, you can do it."

"Anything is possible," said her dad.

Michelle worked hard. But still, sometimes people told her not to aim too high. They said she would never achieve something big because "she was just a Black girl from the South Side of Chicago."

But Michelle chose to listen to her parents. "Anything is possible," she thought. So she graduated from Harvard Law School and became a lawyer at a big firm. One day, her boss asked her to mentor a young lawyer. His name was Barack Hussein Obama.

They fell in love and got married a few years later.

Eventually, Barack told her he wanted to become president of the United States. At first, she thought he was crazy, but then she remembered: "If it can be done, you can do it." So she quit her job and helped him on his campaign.

Barack won the election, and Michelle became the first Black First Lady of the United States. "No one is born smart," she likes to point out. "All of that comes with a lot of hard work."

BORN JANUARY 17, 1964
UNITED STATES OF AMERICA

"ALWAYS STAY TRUE TO YOURSELF AND
NEVER LET WHAT SOMEBODY ELSE SAYS
DISTRACT YOU FROM YOUR GOALS."
—MICHELLE OBAMA

OPRAH WINFREY

TV HOST AND BUSINESSWOMAN

Once there was a little girl who interviewed crows. She also interviewed her corncob dolls. And she was so good at reciting from the Bible that people nicknamed her the Preacher.

Her name was Oprah, and she loved to talk. But her family didn't listen. Her mother brushed her away, saying, "Be quiet! I don't have time for you." Her grandmother never let her cry. "People will think you're weak," she said.

But keeping everything bottled up inside was unbearable.

So Oprah kept looking for opportunities to speak out. She looked for people who would listen to what she had to say. First, she joined the public speaking team in high school. Then she took a job at a local radio station. Eventually, she joined a Baltimore TV news show as a co-anchor.

Her family and friends were excited. But deep inside, Oprah wasn't sure that reporting the news was what she loved the most. She was fired from the show and given a low-rated early morning talk show.

Oprah thought her career was over. Instead, while interviewing an ice cream seller, she discovered her greatest talent: connecting with compassion. People started to love the show because she really listened to her guests. If they cried, she felt their sadness. If they were angry, she understood their pain. And if they were happy, she laughed with them.

Oprah became the queen of talk shows. She moved on to national television. She launched her own TV network and became a multi-billionaire and one of the most generous philanthropists in history.

BORN JANUARY 29, 1954
UNITED STATES OF AMERICA

"YOU GET IN LIFE
WHAT YOU HAVE
THE COURAGE
TO ASK FOR."
—OPRAH WINFREY

ILLUSTRATION BY
T.S. ABE

PAT SUMMITT

BASKETBALL COACH

There once was a girl named Pat who was tough as nails. She grew up on a dairy farm in Tennessee. She worked hard, tending the crops and animals with her four siblings. She also played hard, shooting basketballs in the hayloft.

Pat was really skilled at basketball. By the time she was in third grade, she was playing on the eighth-grade team. In college, she toured around the world. But just before the 1976 Olympics, Pat hurt her knee so badly that a surgeon said her career was done.

"That doctor's crazy as heck if he thinks I'm not going to play ball again!" said Pat. She went to the Olympics and earned her team a silver medal.

At twenty-one, she became head coach of the women's basketball team at the University of Tennessee. Pat's love of the game and her intense work ethic made her unstoppable. She tracked every play and every recruit—even while she was giving birth to her son!

Pat was strict with her team. She believed that every game was important and every player had a chance to be amazing. If they didn't try their hardest, she gave them an icy stare. She also wrote them beautiful letters of motivation, telling them that she believed in them and that they should never give up. "I'm proud to be your coach," she wrote.

Under her leadership, the team won game after game. She racked up 1,098 wins, eight college championships, and a team gold in the 1984 Olympics. Pat won many awards, including the Presidential Medal of Freedom. And, when she retired in 2012, she had the most wins of any women's basketball coach in the history of the NCAA, an organization for college athletes.

JUNE 14, 1952–JUNE 28, 2016
UNITED STATES OF AMERICA

ILLUSTRATION BY
JACQUELYN B. MOORE

"IF I'M NOT
LEADING BY
EXAMPLE, THEN
I'M NOT DOING
THE RIGHT THING."
—PAT SUMMITT

RIGOBERTA MENCHÚ TUM

POLITICAL ACTIVIST

Once there was a girl who was told she didn't matter. She lived high in the mountains of Guatemala. But she and her family had to work down in the valleys picking coffee beans. The plantation owners worked them hard and beat them if they did not pick fast enough. The workers were treated like slaves. They were paid hardly anything. "Your life is not worth a bag of beans," her bosses told her.

"My name is Rigoberta," she replied, "and my life is worth just as much as yours."

Rigoberta was proud of her people and her culture. The Mayans of Guatemala could trace their history back to ancient times. They had a rich and wonderful civilization. But they had been forced into poverty. They were beaten and even killed by soldiers if they dared to protest.

She started fighting for better conditions and equal rights for her people. She organized strikes and demonstrations. Although Rigoberta could not read or write, she spoke with conviction. More and more people joined her cause. Many were taken away and killed, including Rigoberta's own parents and her brother. The government tried to silence her. Local landowners tried to break her, but no one could crush her fearless spirit. She insisted on telling her story—not because it was hers but because it was the story of oppressed Indigenous peoples everywhere.

Rigoberta played a large part in ending the civil war in Guatemala. For this and for her life's work campaigning for the rights of the poor, she was awarded the Nobel Peace Prize.

BORN JANUARY 9, 1959

GUATEMALA

ILLUSTRATION BY
DEBORA GUIDI

"I AM LIKE A DROP OF WATER ON A ROCK.
AFTER DRIP, DRIP, DRIPPING IN THE SAME PLACE,
I BEGIN TO LEAVE A MARK, AND I LEAVE MY MARK
IN MANY PEOPLE'S HEARTS."
—RIGOBERTA MENCHÚ TUM

RUTH BADER GINSBURG

SUPREME COURT JUSTICE

Once upon a time, there was a girl who dreamed of becoming a great lawyer. "A lady lawyer?" people would mock her. "Don't be ridiculous! Lawyers and judges are always men."

Ruth looked around her and saw that they were right. "But there's no reason why that shouldn't change," she thought to herself.

She attended Harvard Law School and Columbia Law School as one of their brightest students.

Her husband, Marty, was also a student at Harvard. "Your wife should be home baking cookies and looking after the baby," people used to say. But Marty didn't listen. Ruth was a terrible cook! And besides, he loved taking care of their daughter. He was proud of his brilliant wife.

Ruth was passionate about women's rights. She argued six landmark cases on gender equality before the United States Supreme Court. Then she became the second female Supreme Court justice in the country's history.

There are nine justices on the Supreme Court. "If I'm asked, when will there be enough women on the Supreme Court?, I say, 'When there are nine,'" she said. "People are shocked—but there've been nine men, like forever, and nobody's ever raised their eyebrows at that."

Ruth never let anything get in the way of her important job on the Supreme Court. Despite her many battles with cancer and multiple surgeries, Ruth rarely missed a day in court—even in her eighties! Ruth was also a style icon, thanks to the extravagant collars she wore in court with her judge's robes.

MARCH 15, 1933–SEPTEMBER 18, 2020
UNITED STATES OF AMERICA

ILLUSTRATION BY
ELEANOR DAVIS

"I DISSENT."
—RUTH BADER GINSBURG

SONIA SOTOMAYOR

SUPREME COURT JUSTICE

Once there was a girl who wanted to be a detective. Her name was Sonia.

When she was six, Sonia was diagnosed with diabetes. "You can't be a detective," she was told. "You need to find something else!" But Sonia didn't give up. Her favorite TV show was a legal drama starring a brilliant lawyer named Perry Mason. He wasn't as exciting as her favorite detective, Nancy Drew, but he was great at solving crimes.

"Fair enough," she thought. "I'll be a lawyer like Perry Mason."

Sonia came from a poor family that had moved to New York from Puerto Rico. When she was nine, her father died, leaving her mother to provide for the entire family. She worked six days a week, and she kept telling Sonia that she had to get an excellent education.

Sonia didn't disappoint her. She studied hard and became one of the few Hispanic women accepted by Princeton University at that time. "I felt like an alien," she later recalled. But she still managed to graduate with top grades, and she continued her studies at the prestigious Yale Law School.

She became a judge and worked at every level of the judicial system. When Barack Obama was elected president, he nominated Sonia to the highest court of the United States. In 2009, she became the first Latina to serve on the Supreme Court.

Sonia played a major role in some of the country's most important legal cases, including the historic decision to make same-sex marriage legal in all states.

BORN JUNE 25, 1954
UNITED STATES OF AMERICA

ILLUSTRATION BY
KATHRIN HONESTA

"THE LATINA IN ME IS AN EMBER
THAT BLAZES FOREVER."
—SONIA SOTOMAYOR

STACEY ABRAMS

ACTIVIST AND POLITICIAN

Once there was a girl named Stacey who loved hip-hop, *Star Trek*, and climbing trees. She was one of six children, and her parents couldn't always afford electricity. Still, her family showed up for school, church, and volunteering at soup kitchens. They believed there was always a way to help others.

Stacey got the highest grades. She was named valedictorian of her high school. Part of her prize was a visit with the governor. He lived in a mansion with huge gates and a guard who said Stacey didn't belong there. She didn't know if he said that because she had brown skin or because she looked poor. She didn't care what his reason was. She just knew, from that moment on, that she wanted "to be the person who got to open the gates."

Stacey earned a law degree, wrote novels, started two small businesses, and became a lawmaker in Georgia. She devoted herself to fighting poverty, making public schools stronger, protecting women's rights, and helping military families. In 2018, Stacey ran for governor of Georgia. She was the first Black woman to do this for a major political party. She got more votes than any other Democrat in the state's history. But her opponent made sure that a lot of people weren't allowed to vote, and Stacey lost.

Stacey didn't quit. She remembered that guard trying to block her from the governor's mansion years ago and channeled her frustration into inspiration. Over the next two years, she dedicated herself to making voting easier. She also registered 800,000 voters in Georgia—because she believes that everyone's voice matters, and she will open those gates for all.

BORN DECEMBER 9, 1973
UNITED STATES OF AMERICA

"LEADERSHIP IS ABOUT ANSWERING THAT QUESTION: HOW CAN I HELP?"
—STACEY ABRAMS

ILLUSTRATION BY KELSEE THOMAS

TAMMY DUCKWORTH

SENATOR

Once there was a girl who dreamed of serving her country. But over the first sixteen years of her life, Tammy lived in five different countries: Thailand, Indonesia, Cambodia, Singapore, and the United States.

It wasn't a glamorous life. Tammy's family finally settled in Hawaii. But her father couldn't get a job, and her mother wasn't allowed to enter the country. It took six months and lots of paperwork before the family was reunited.

Tammy's father was a US Marine during World War II. When Tammy grew up, she joined the military, too. She trained as a helicopter pilot. In 2004, she was sent to Iraq with the US Army. One day, Tammy's helicopter was hit by a grenade. She was badly injured and lost both legs. The army awarded her a Purple Heart, a special medal given to soldiers who are injured in war.

Tammy's life looked different after her injury. But she also discovered a new purpose. She started working to improve the lives of her fellow military veterans. In 2012, Tammy was elected to the US House of Representatives. And four years later, she ran for Senate and won.

Tammy was the first disabled woman and only the second Asian American woman to be elected to the Senate. In 2018, she became the first senator to give birth while in office. She even brought her newborn daughter with her to cast a vote on the Senate floor while she was on maternity leave. "It doesn't matter if I am tired," Tammy said. "I am going to show up every day and fight."

BORN MARCH 12, 1968
UNITED STATES OF AMERICA

"I SHOULDN'T EVEN BE HERE. SO IF I'M HERE, I BETTER DO SOMETHING GOOD."
—TAMMY DUCKWORTH

ILLUSTRATION BY
ALESSANDRA DE CRISTOFARO

WILMA MANKILLER

TRIBAL CHIEF

Once there was a girl named Wilma who believed everyone deserves a home. Wilma was born in Tahlequah, Oklahoma, the capital of the Cherokee Nation. Wilma grew up poor with ten brothers and sisters. When she was little, her family moved to California. The government promised they would find money and jobs there. But that never happened, and Wilma felt betrayed.

The Cherokee people, like many Native Americans, had been relocated before by the United States government. They were also robbed of their lands, abused, and even killed throughout history. Wilma felt like she had to do something to help her people.

She went to school, got married, and started a family. When she told her husband she wanted to be an activist for social justice, he disapproved. So she divorced him and moved with her two young daughters back to Oklahoma. Their home had no running water or electricity. But they were happy to be back on their homeland.

Wilma had many setbacks. She was in a serious car accident. She found out she had a disease that affected her muscles. It made it hard to even hold a pencil. Still, Wilma focused on the power of *gadugi*, which is a Cherokee word for "shared effort." Wilma rallied people together. They rebuilt homes and dug miles of ditches so pipes could bring water to their community.

In 1985, she became the first woman to serve as principal chief of the Cherokee Nation. She led her people with dignity and hope. She fought for all Native Americans to get healthcare, education, and respect. "I want to be remembered as the person who helped us restore faith in ourselves," she said.

NOVEMBER 18, 1945–APRIL 6, 2010
UNITED STATES OF AMERICA

"THE MOST FULFILLED PEOPLE ARE THE ONES WHO GET UP EVERY MORNING AND STAND FOR SOMETHING LARGER THAN THEMSELVES."
—WILMA MANKILLER

ILLUSTRATION BY ALEXANDRA BOWMAN

XIYE BASTIDA

CLIMATE ACTIVIST

Once upon a time, a terrible drought gripped Xiye's hometown of San Pedro Tultepec, Mexico. The land was parched. The lake dried up. Crops died. After two years, the rain finally came—but it wasn't a normal storm. It poured and poured until the land flooded.

Xiye belonged to the Otomi Toltec, a nation of Indigenous people. Her community understood the importance of living in balance with the environment and caring for the Earth.

When Xiye moved with her family to New York City, she saw that it was damaged as well. A huge storm had hit a few years before, and she realized the balance was dangerously off. The climate was in crisis. She had to do something to make it right.

In March 2019, when she was seventeen years old, Xiye organized a strike at her high school. Under her leadership, about six hundred students walked out of class. They demanded that governments take action to stop climate change and protect the planet. Months later, Xiye and other young activists around the world led a week of global strikes and protests for climate action and Indigenous rights.

To make time for her activism, Xiye had to give up gymnastics and other activities she loved. But the Earth was worth it.

"Indigenous people have been taking care of the Earth for thousands of years because that is their culture," Xiye said. "For me, being an environmental activist and a climate justice activist is not a hobby. It's a way of life."

BORN APRIL 18, 2002

UNITED STATES OF AMERICA

"EARTH IS OUR HOME. IT GIVES YOU AIR, WATER, AND SHELTER. EVERYTHING WE NEED. ALL IT ASKS IS THAT WE PROTECT IT."
—XIYE BASTIDA

ILLUSTRATION BY
SALLY DENG

WRITE YOUR STORY

_____

_____

_____

_____

_____

_____

_____

_____

_____

_____

_____

_____

_____

_____

_____

_____

_____

_____

_____

DRAW YOUR PORTRAIT

WHAT KIND OF LEADER ARE YOU?

You, yes YOU, are a leader. Whether you are loud or quiet, you already have the qualities inside you to change the world. Take this quiz to find out what kind of leader you are!

1. WHEN FACED WITH AN ISSUE, HOW DO YOU SOLVE IT?

A. I draft a petition and draw my protest sign.

B. I rally my troops and take my enemies down by any means necessary.

C. I always solve my problems peacefully and with a cool head.

2. WHICH DESCRIPTION SOUNDS MOST LIKE YOU?

A. I'm passionate, loud, and feisty.

B. I'm strong, courageous, and disciplined.

C. I'm well spoken, fair, and caring.

3. WHERE WOULD YOU LIKE TO LIVE?

A. Anywhere is fine as long as I have a roof over my head. I don't need much.

B. A quiet castle on the side of a cliff

C. A modern house with too many rooms to count

4. WHAT'S YOUR FAVORITE FOOD?

A. Something organic and environmentally friendly

B. Pie. Definitely pie.

C. Something fancy from another culture

5. WHAT DO YOU WISH YOU WERE WEARING RIGHT NOW?

    A. A Rebel Girls T-shirt and ripped jeans

    B. Full body armor

    C. A pantsuit or judge's robes

6. YOU'RE GOING ON AN ADVENTURE! WHERE WILL YOU GO?

    A. A country or neighborhood less fortunate than mine

    B. Somewhere challenging, like a mountain, desert, or forest

    C. A tropical island paradise

7. WHAT AFTER-SCHOOL CLUB WOULD YOU LOVE TO JOIN?

    A. Something creative, like drama club, choir, or art class

    B. Any sports team—fencing, lacrosse, soccer, tennis—I love them all!

    C. The debate team or Model UN

8. HOW DO YOU MAKE DECISIONS?

    A. I follow my heart and the passionate people I care about.

    B. It's an even mix between my head and heart.

    C. I follow my head and consider the facts.

9. WHAT'S YOUR WEAPON OF CHOICE?

    A. The power of the people!

    B. A sword or spear

    C. My voice and my pen

10. YOU'VE BEEN TRANSPORTED INTO A FAIRY TALE! WHICH CHARACTER WOULD YOU BE?

    A. The peasant farmer leading a revolt

    B. The hero saving the day

    C. The wise old tree giving advice

Check out your answers on page 60!

ANSWERS TO
"WHAT KIND OF LEADER ARE YOU?"

✓ MOSTLY A'S

You're the Ardent Activist! Your fiery passion mobilizes large groups of people into action that shakes governments and social systems. You might be found at a protest march waving a creative sign about what you believe in or shouting through a bullhorn with your fist in the air.

✓ MOSTLY B'S

You're the Warrior! You want to protect your people and ensure their continued survival. Your focus and determination are impressive. You can be intense, but you just care deeply about your community's safety.

✓ MOSTLY C'S

You're the Stately Politician! You are wise beyond your years, and you use your knowledge to advise, guide, and coach others around you. You give heartfelt speeches full of fire and passion. Each word you speak carries power.

LEADERSHIP TRAINING

Leaders are powerful. They have to make decisions that impact others. To do this, they must decide what they believe in, what they support, and who they are. Try the activities below to hone your leadership skills!

EXERCISE 1: MATCH YOUR SKILLS TO YOUR CAUSE

You know you want to leave the world better than you found it. But what can you do to change the world? Grab a pen and a notebook and explore your answers to these questions.

1. Are you a writer, a singer, or an artist? Do you enjoy speaking in front of others? Make a list of the things you do well.
2. From anti-bullying to climate justice, there are many causes in the world today. Which causes are most important to you? Why?
3. Think of all the ways you can put your talents to use for your favorite causes. Write them down.

EXERCISE 2: TELL THE WORLD HOW YOU FEEL

Practice your powers of persuasion. You can use your words in many ways. Choose a type of writing and give it a try!

1. Pick a style of writing: protest song, protest poem, speech to your classmates, letter to the editor (of a newspaper or online publication), letter to your elected representative.
2. In the style you chose, write about an issue that means a lot to you. Be clear. Be persuasive. Use your words to convince others to join with you in your cause.
3. Talk to your grown-ups about how you might share your song, poem, speech, or letter with others.

EXERCISE 3: GET READY TO PROTEST!

It's never too early to prepare for a demonstration! Get your signs and slogans ready!

1. A slogan is a quick, catchy phrase that gets your point across. Brainstorm a strong slogan for each cause you believe in. Pick a slogan to put on a sign.
2. Find a big piece of cardboard to use for your protest sign. (Ask a grown-up before you start cutting up boxes!) Remember: protest signs work best when people can read them from far away. Write your slogan in big letters. Add colors or drawings to illustrate your argument.

EXERCISE 4: FIND THE LEADER IN YOU

The women in these stories exhibit leadership in different ways. You can learn a lot by imagining yourself in their shoes. Write down your answers or practice them aloud.

1. Picture yourself at the Olympics. Like Aly Raisman, you are the gymnastics team captain. Your teammate is freaking out. Before she gets on the balance beam, what do you say to calm her and keep her focused?
2. As the mayor of a small island like Giusi Nicolini, you have to make a lot of tough decisions. If refugees began arriving on your beaches, what would you do? Would you let them land? Or send them away? How would you explain your decision to the people of your town?
3. As a young woman, Michelle Obama got great advice from her parents. "If it can be done, you can do it," her mother said. What is the best advice you've ever gotten? What advice would you like to give to the world?
4. Stacey Abrams dedicates her time to educating people about voting and making sure they are able to vote. Imagine working with Stacey. You meet someone who is not registered to vote. What do you say to convince them that voting is important?

READ MORE

Some of the stories in this book come from different editions of *Good Night Stories for Rebel Girls*. For more stories, check out these books:

THE ILLUSTRATORS

Twenty-five extraordinary female artists from all over the world illustrated the portraits in this book. Here are their names.

AISHA AKEJU, USA, 23

ALESSANDRA DE CRISTOFARO, ITALY, 51

ALEXANDRA BOWMAN, USA, 53

ANA GALVAÑ, SPAIN, 15

ANNALISA VENTURA, ITALY, 35

CINDY ECHEVARRIA, USA, 11

DEBORA GUIDI, ITALY, 43

ELEANOR DAVIS, USA, 45

ELENIA BERETTA, ITALY, 9

FANESHA FABRE, USA, 33

JACQUELYN B. MOORE, USA, 41

KATHRIN HONESTA, INDONESIA, 47

KELSEE THOMAS, USA, 49

KIKI LJUNG, SPAIN, 13

LAURA PÉREZ, SPAIN, 19

MARTA SIGNORI, ITALY, 37

NICOLE MILES, THE BAHAMAS, 25

PAOLA ROLLO, ITALY, 17

SALINI PERERA, CANADA, 7

SALLY DENG, USA, 55

SALLY NIXON, USA, 21

SARA BONDI, ITALY, 31

SARAH MADDEN, UK, 27

T.S. ABE, UK, 39

THANDIWE TSHABALALA, SOUTH AFRICA, 29

ABOUT REBEL GIRLS

REBEL GIRLS is a global, multi-platform edutainment brand, dedicated to inspiring and instilling confidence in a generation of girls around the world. Born from a 2016 best-selling children's book, Rebel Girls teaches girls about real-life, diverse, and extraordinary women throughout history, whose stories are brought to life by a coalition of equally amazing women (and men!). In addition to an award-winning book series, podcast, virtual experiences, and toys, the company is expanding its reach to television, live theater, and a digital app. Its community of self-identified Rebel Girls spans more than 85 countries, with 6.5 million books sold in 49 languages and 10 million podcast downloads.

Join the Rebel Girls' community:
- ✦ Facebook: facebook.com/rebelgirls
- ✦ Instagram: @rebelgirls
- ✦ Twitter: @rebelgirlsbook
- ✦ Web: rebelgirls.com
- ✦ Podcast: rebelgirls.com/podcast

If you liked this book, please take a moment to review it wherever you prefer!